The Burn Game

The Burn Game

101 ways
to burn your buds

Bozo #2

authorHOUSE®

AuthorHouse™
1663 Liberty Drive
Bloomington, IN 47403
www.authorhouse.com
Phone: 1-800-839-8640

Published by AuthorHouse   03/19/2012

ISBN: 978-1-4685-5327-7 (sc)
ISBN: 978-1-4685-5326-0 (e)

Library of Congress Control Number: 2012902988

Any people depicted in stock imagery provided by Thinkstock are models, and such images are being used for illustrative purposes only.
Certain stock imagery © Thinkstock.

This book is printed on acid-free paper.

Because of the dynamic nature of the Internet, any web addresses or links contained in this book may have changed since publication and may no longer be valid. The views expressed in this work are solely those of the author and do not necessarily reflect the views of the publisher, and the publisher hereby disclaims any responsibility for them.

Preface

There are several assumptions of how the sport of "burning" began. Many believe that it is a natural behavior pattern in the male human species dating back to, as early as, the caveman era. As a young man reaches his early stages of adulthood, he can often develop an overwhelming desire to compete in various social events and games. Although many may consider such games to be juvenile and decadent, it is also a belief of many that such games are a crucial element in the development of one's masculinity and social prowess.

Never the less, young men over the years have become more and more precise in their attacks on peers in their attempts to ascend the ladder of manhood. The old saying "boys will be boys", can be heard ever present in every school hallway, summer camps, military barrack, inmate housing unit, or sports locker room.

In recent years, the "Burn Game" has become somewhat of an underground favorite among adolescents, as well as up-to-date elder males that strive to stay in touch with their more youthful counterparts, for establishing a sense of camaraderie amongst each other. The reason for this is suspected to be that the "Burn Game" requires no equipment, has no time limit, and literally requires no verbal communication. This means that the playing field is universal, and that the "Burn Game" can virtually be executed anywhere in the world.

This book was written in hopes to enlighten those with less knowledge of the game and to help portray some insight why it has become such a popular pass-time of the male human species.

Chapter 1

1st Degree Burns

"Accidental"

The accidental burn is any burn that is not planned by an intending arsonist. Accidentals most commonly occur in a gym or school locker room, where an unknowing arsonist is stepping out from a shower and is oblivious to who is in their surrounding area.

"Accomplice" *

Points are rewarded to an accomplice for aiding in the set-up of a burn attack. The accomplice gains points for only his help in the attack, while the arsonist will gain points for the original method of the attack as well as the combo points for having an accomplice.

"Batwing"

With the testicle sack in a warm state, so that the skin is loose and permeable, the arsonist grabs the left portion of his testicle skin with the left hand and the right portion of his testicle skin with his right hand. He then stretches the skin upwards and out to display a flat and veiny area of skin resembling that of a bat's wing.

"Brain"

To complete this attack, the arsonist must stretch the testicle skin upwards, completely covering the penis, so that the visibly exposed skin of the testicles resembles the shape of a human brain. This pose can prove to be a difficult task for one with a large penis, as they may not have sufficient testicle skin to fully conceal.

"Bubble Gum"

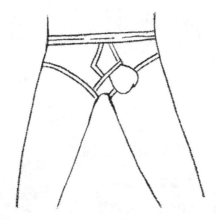

"Bubble Gum" is a very simple, but effective burn. The arsonist simply unzips his pants or opens the slot in his underwear, then lets the testicles rest on his lap, resembling a large wad of bubble gum that has dropped from someone's mouth.

"Bunk Mate" *

Mates/Inmates that share the same bunk are eligible for bonus combo points for burning the other while in bed. The arsonist calls to his bunk mate/victim that he has something interesting to show him. As the victim comes to investigate, he is greeted with a surprise burn of the other bunk mate's choice.

"Castration"

The arsonist tucks his testicles between his legs, revealing only the penis, so that from the front view, it looks as if he has had his testicles removed. This can be very uncomfortable, and even impossible for those with smaller than average sized testicles.

"Coat Hanger", "Clothes Line", "Hat Rack"

The arsonist uses his erect penis to hang garments such as clothes, wash cloths, towels, hats, coats, etc. This is one of the very few occasions in which neither the testicle or penis skin has to be visible in order to inflict a burn.

"Concealed Weapon"

With his penis in full-chub mode, the arsonist cuts a hole in the pocket of his pants. He then places the head and the shaft of the penis through the hole. While his erect penis is still hidden inside the pocket of his pants, he then seeks out his victim and proceeds to ask "would you like to see my new gun?" When the victim jubilantly replies "yes", the arsonist then pulls down the pocket of his pants, revealing his throbbing manhood, leaving the unsuspecting victim with a first degee burn.

"Dime-bag"

A specific penis mode is irrelevant in this attack, but sports mode will likely be the mode of choice for its ease to obtain. In this pose the arsonist must reduce his body temperature so that the testicles shrink, and draw upwards into the sack, dramatically reducing the size of the sack. After maximum shrinkage has been achieved, he then grasps the penis with one hand and holds it in an upward position so that only a dime-bag sized pair of testicles are revealed to the victim.

"Drive By" *

A "drive-by" burn situation can occur anytime that an arsonist executes an attack from a moving vehicle. (Car, Bicycle, Moped, etc.)

"Goat"

This technique is widely used because of its quickness and ease of execution. The arsonist simply turns his back to the victim, drops his pants to the ground, then bends over to reveal a hairy anal crevice, coupled with a rear view of his testicles and penis dangling below.

"Guitar Hero"

In full-chub mode, the arsonist grasps the penis shaft with an underhand grip in the same manner that a guitarist would grasp the neck of his instrument. With his opposite hand, he pretends to strum the testicle sack with a pick, as if strumming the strings on a guitar. Rapid finger movements along the shaft of the penis will help to further accentuate this technique.

"Hemorrhoid"

The hemorrhoid is basically the rearview of the "Mangina" pose. With the penis and testicles tucked between both legs, a rear sighting reveals a hemorrhoid-like mass dangling just below the anal cavity.

"Hernia"

Although not a very comfortable burn to execute, this pose has become very popular for its stealth nature and quickness to obtain. With his pants zipped, buttoned, and in the "up" position, the arsonist grabs one testicle and stretches it upward towards the top of his pants so that the waistline keeps the single testicle suspended outside of the pants, resembling an abdominal hernia.

"Instant Replay" *

Instant replay allows an arsonist to gain bonus combo points for burning the same victim, using the same burn method within a window of five minutes. For each consecutive replay, the arsonist will accrue five additional bonus points to the points that he has already gained by the specific burn.

"Joust"

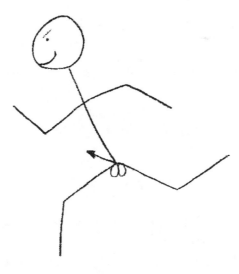

With full-chub mode engaged, the arsonist simply drops whatever clothing that he is wearing to cover his erection, and charges fiercely into the area of whom he is trying to victimize, as if he were a knight engaging battle with his jousting stick.

"Lasso"

In either flaccid or semi-chub mode, the arsonist grabs his penis at the base, turns so that his side is facing the intended victim, and begins to twirl his penis towards the victim as a cowboy would twirl a lasso at his cattle.

"Mangina"

Made world famous by Wild Bill in the movie "Silence of the Lambs". Simply tuck the penis and the testicles between both legs, and close both legs together. This gives a frontal illusion that there is no penis or testicles. Also, there is usually a fold of skin left in the crotch area that resembles a woman's bare vagina

"Messenger" *

This technique is used to get the attention of a desired victim. The arsonist recruits a messenger to approach the victim and inform them that someone is trying to get their attention to tell them something. When the victim turns to look in the instructed direction, he is burned by the arsonist, who has already struck his desired pose. Combo points are earned by the arsonist while the messenger collects his share for the assist.

"Mirror Effect" *

The arsonist uses a strategically placed mirror to relay a pose into the unsuspecting victim's line of sight.

"Money Bag"

This technique can be used in any mode desired, but is most commonly executed in the "flacid" mode. The reason for this is that the testicles need to be warm and relaxed so that they may hang as low as possible. Once an acceptable low-hang has been achieved, the arsonist simply grabs the testicle sack at the base of the penis and holds it so that the lower portion of the testicles is still visible, dangling from the bottom side of his hand, as would be a bag of money.

"Ninja Slipper"

This is one of the only poses that can inflict a burn without actually showing any genital skin. With the penis in full-chub mode, the arsonist hikes his pants up so that they are excessively tight in the crotch region, revealing a distinct outline of his erect penis.

"Neck Tie", "Bow Tie"

The arsonist while in full-chub mode, ties a neck/bow tie around the shaft of his penis as he would his neck when dressing for a formal event.

"Over The Counter"

No prescription needed for this one. In any mode desired, the arsonist places his penis on the countertop, in plain view, and waits for his unsuspecting victim to visually discover.

"Pig In A Blanket", "Sausage Wrap"

In any mode desired, the arsonist wraps the left testicle around the left side of the penis, and the right testicle around the right side so that only the head of the penis is still visible. This may prove to be a difficult attack for those with insufficient testicle skin.

"Racist" *

An arsonist is rewarded additional combo points for burning a victim of a different race or nationality.

"Sniper" *

The "Sniper" attack can be a convenient method when the desired victim is in a less than desirable surrounding to inflict a burn. The arsonist gets into his chosen pose and either waits until the victim spots him, or he may choose to implement the "Messenger" technique, thus gaining extra combo points. To be considered a sniper, the arsonist must be at a distance of at least 100 feet, or a minimum of one floor/building level away from the intended victim at the time of the burn.

"Squirrel Trampoline"

With the penis in flaccid or semi-chub mode, the arsonist stretches out his testicle skin to form a horizontal surface. He then bounces his penis up and down off of the testicle skin, simulating a squirrel bouncing on a trampoline.

"Stage Fright" *

Very simple to execute in cold weather, this is just a standard sports mode pose, where the penis and testicles have reduced drastically in size usually as the result of colder than normal temperatures. This attack must be executed on some type of raised platform to be eligible for "stage fright" combo points.

"Sub-Zero" *

A burn attack which is executed at a temperature below zero degrees Fahrenheit.

"Swollen Thumb"

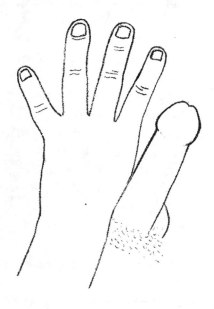

With the penis in semi-chub mode, the arsonist tucks his thumb under the bottom side of his hand so that it is no longer visible from the top side. He then places his hand beside his penis so that the penis takes the place of where the thumb would normally be, creating the illusion that the penis IS the thumb, but swollen, as if a carpenter had missed a nail with his hammer, hitting his thumb instead.

"Text Message" *

This new age of technology has now enabled us to inflict burns via cellular phone text message. The arsonist takes a picture of himself in his pose of choice, and then sends it in a picture-text to his desired victim. By the time that the victim downloads the message along with the picture, and realizes what he has opened, it is too late. He has already been set ablaze.

"Thimble", "Sports Mode", "Shy Boy", "Knubby",

Different terms for a standard extreme sports mode attack. Maximum shrinkage of the penis is achieved during this attack.

"Urinary"

An Arsonist burns his victim while urinating. This method tends to be unintentional, on most occasions, but is never-the-less worthy of points.

"Virgin" *

This method refers to a first time burn executed by an arsonist. He will gain bonus combo points, in addition to his original points awarded for his specific attack, if the victim has never been burned before. Arsonists are also eligible for "virgin" burn points if it is their first time executing any form of burn attack.

"White-Head"

With the penis in flaccid mode, the arsonist strips down to his underwear and reveals only the head of his penis through the urination slot. This method can only be executed naturally by white males. Other males may attempt via usage of body paint.

Chapter 2

2nd Degree Burns

"Bentley"

This method can only be executed by an arsonist that has a natural curvature in his penis while in full-chub mode. He simply obtains an erection and burns away.

"Birth Mark" *

The arsonist, using body paint, paints his penis the opposite shade of his natural skin tone. He then asks his intended victim, "Would you like to see my birthmark?" When the victim replies "yes", the arsonist engages his attack, scoring him a second degree burn.

"Bobbit"

This can prove to be one of the more difficult and uncomfortable poses to execute. The arsonist must stretch the penis around the testicles and tuck it between his legs. This is similar to the "Mangina" technique, but in this pose the testicles remain visible from the front view, projecting an illusion that the penis has been removed as in the case of a well-known incident that occurred in the mid 90's. Perpetrators with insufficient penis length may have trouble executing this pose.

"Boogy Man" *

The arsonist stands in the victim's bedroom closet, waiting in the pose of his choice. As the victim opens the door to grab his garments, he is delivered a frightening burn that he will not soon forget. Childhood fears become a painful reality in the form of the "Boogy Man" burn.

"Cook Out"

The gathering of acquaintances to enjoy a nice, warm, sunny afternoon of backyard grilling can invoke many opportunities for a seasoned arsonist to exploit his craft. One of the most coveted attacks in this situation is the "Cook Out" burn. After a friend accepts an offer of a hotdog, the arsonist begins to pretend to prepare the bun. However, instead of adding condiments and the normal weiner of choice, the arsonist fills the bun with his very own brand of meat . . . . MAN-MEAT! He wraps the empty bun around the shaft of his penis, still attached to his body, and keeps his back towards his victim until the final moment when he serves his pal with a meal that he will not soon forget.

"Cousin It"

Very much like the "Castration" pose in that the testicles are tucked between the legs, revealing only a flaccid penis, but surrounded by an extremely large amount of pubic hair.

"Curtis Lowe" *

This method of attack is mainly limited to older black men, with white pubic hair, as the name was popularized by a 1970's southern rock ballad. The arsonist simply executes any burn attack of his choosing, but also gains valuable combo points for having the correct skin tone and pubic hair color. Although normally only a select few are capable of executing this combo, skin paint and a white crotch wig can be used to imitate the requirements of this technique.

"Cyclops"

This method resembles the "Hemorrhoid" but the penis and testicles are turned so that, from the rearview, the penis is in front of the testicles, giving the illusion that the penis is a nose, the testicles are the nostrils, and the anal cavity represents the single eye of the Greek titan "Cyclops".

"Dingleberry"

With the arsonist's back facing toward the intended victim, he begins to squat while holding his penis up, so that it is not visible from his back side. With the testicles warm and hanging as low as possible, he proceeds to do a slight wiggle/shimmy, so that his testicles bounce and swing back and forth, resembling that of a dingleberry, which to those unknowing, is a lump of feces tangled and suspended in the pubic hairs of the anal crevice.

"Door Stop"

While anticipating the entrance of a victim into a closed room, the arsonist, in full-chub mode, stands against the wall in the area where he would be directly behind the door, if it were to be opened, with his back-side facing the wall. The unsuspecting victim then opens the door to enter the room. As he turns to shut the door behind him, the arsonist reveals to him a human door-stop, in the form of an erect penis.

"Double Barrel" *

A team effort is required for this method. Two arsonists work themselves into semi-chub or full-chub mode. Then, while standing hip to hip beside each other, and facing their intended victim/victims, they point their penis at them, giving the simulation that they are staring down the barrel of a double-barreled shotgun.

"Double Salute" *

A soldier or law official, can obtain points for a double salute if he can manage to maintain a visible, full-chub mode attack while saluting a higher ranking officer.

"Double Vision" *

A double vision burn can be credited when two arsonists burn the same victim/victims simultaneously, while using identical burn methods. Combo bonus points are collected in addition to the standard points rewarded for the chosen attack.

"Dude Looks Like A Lady" *

A burn attack in which the arsonist is disguised as a female. (Transvestite, Hermaphrodite, Halloween Costume, etc.)

"Dude Love"

A popular burn method that is widely used in the gay community. An arsonist can gain points for "dude love" attacks anytime that a victim sees the arsonist's penis touch another man's skin. For safety reasons, this method is usually attempted with the consent of his accomplice, thus generating additional combo bonus points.

"Eye Of The Tiger", "Zebra"

In semi-chub or full-chub mode, the arsonist, using body paint, colors his penis so that it is striped like a tiger or zebra. To be eligible for "eye of the tiger" credit, the arsonist's urination hole must be pointing directly at the eye of his intended victim.

"Green Thumb"

This method is executed in the same manner as the "swollen thumb" technique, with the exception that the penis is colored green via body paint.

"Houdini"

The arsonist tucks his penis and testicles between his legs, as noted in the "mangina" method. Then, as the victim hones in on the visual confusion, the arsonist spreads his legs slightly so that his concealed manhood suddenly reappears as if he had performed some sort of magicians trick.

"Hostage" *

In a hostage situation, one burn victim can transfer his burn to another without loosing any points. As long as the arsonist holds his pose, if the first victim can provoke another to look at the pose before it is retracted, victim number two will take the place of the first victim, as if the first victim was being held hostage by the arsonist and was replaced by victim number two. The arsonist will double the point value of his initial attack if he is successful.

"Hulk", "Grinch"

The arsonist uses body paint to color his entire penis green. He then works himself into the most extreme full-chub mode possible, fully extended, with veins extruding all over. At Christmas only, the "Hulk" burn can also be substituted as the "Grinch" burn. However, the Grinch burn can be executed in any mode desired.

"Icarus" *

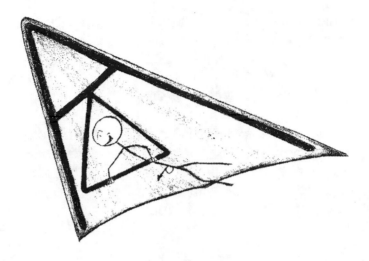

Any burn attack that is executed during flight. The flight time must exceed twenty seconds to validate the attack, which may consist of commercial airlines, private planes, hang-glider, parasailing, helicopter, etc.

"Incest" *

An arsonist becomes eligible for incest burn points by performing an attack on a member of their own immediate family. This includes parents, grand-parents, siblings, aunts, uncles, and first cousins.

"Incubator"

Resembling a rearward view of the "castration" pose, the arsonist tucks his testicles between his legs so that they are positioned just below the anal cavity. He then releases flagellant gas, simulating the same effect that an incubator would have on an egg.

"Jimmy Jacket" *

An arsonist is eligible for "jimmy jacket" points if he successfully inflicts a burn while wearing a condom.

"Lolly-Pop" *

Perhaps the most enjoyable burn method of all to execute. While implementing an accomplice to orally caress his penis, the arsonist strategically lures his victim into witnessing his penis being treated as if it were a lolly-pop by an accomplice of his choosing.

"Nessie"

Executed in any body of water, the arsonist, while in semi-chub or full-chub mode, conceals his entire body under the surface of the water. As the unsuspecting victim visually scans the surface, they initially see nothing out of the ordinary. Then, suddenly, like the legendary monster of Lochness Lake, an erect penis emerges from the surface, scarring them with a second degree burn.

"Nightmare" *

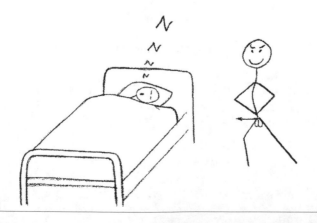

As the victim lies sleeping peacefully, the arsonist strikes a pose and then awakens the victim with a loud noise. The victim then opens his eyes only to be burned by the pose of a well planned attack.

"Raging" *

Raging burn points are rewarded when the arsonist has a rash or break-out in the genital area, usually caused by an S.T.D. or an allergic reaction.

"Sandman" *

The arsonist lures his victim into a dark room. With the lights off, he assumes the position of his desired attack. Then, as the victim scans the room in search of light, the arsonist or his accomplice proceeds to flicker the light switch on and off, creating a strobe effect, much like that which is seen in a popular 90's heavy metal video.

"Sasquatch", "Bin Laden", "Abe Lincoln", "Simba", "Chris Cringle"

Each of these attacks can be executed in any mode desired. To be eligible, the arsonist must be extremely endowed in the department of pubic hair. Either obtained through natural growth or a false disguise via crotch wig, the groin area will resemble a very large human beard, sasquatch, or possibly the mane of an adult male lion. A deviation of white pubic hair invokes the "Chris Cringle" burn, which for those unknowledgeable, is Santa Clause

"Spotter" *

Within the walls of a gymnasium there are several opportunities to score burn points. One of the most commonly used tactics is the "spotter". As the victim is working-out diligently on his chest routine, performing the bench press exercise, he eventually increases the weight to the extent that he needs a spotter's assistance to insure the safety of the movement. The eager arsonist, who has been waiting in suspect of this engagement all along, pounces on the opportunity when the victim invites him to spot. He then walks behind the bench to assume his assisting position. Then suddenly, as the victim lies back on the bench to begin his set, he realizes that he has made a devastating mistake. The helpful colleague that he once thought was there for his safety, was only a well trained arsonist in disguise, burning him intensely with an up-close attack.

"Streaker"

This timeless technique is one that needs no explanation. Great for sporting events, city sidewalks, and hotel hallways, the "Streaker" is a gutsy attack and the arsonist must be prepared to endure legal consequences after the execution. In any mode of choice, the arsonist simply strips down so that his genitals are exposed, and takes off running wherever his instincts carry him.

"Top Dead Center"

This pose is virtually impossible to execute by many. The reason for this is that the arsonist must have sufficient enough penis length. With his penis in full-chub mode, the arsonist must be able to contact his belly-button with the head of his penis. A slight arch in the back may be used to help complete the pose if necessary.

"Tourist"

This technique is great for venues that entertain large crowds such as festivals, concerts, and theme parks. While in disguise as an indulging tourist, the arsonist cuts a hole in the inner side of a fanny pack, which is strapped around his waist. He then inserts his penis into the hole, while keeping the fanny pack zipped to conceal its contents. After the victim accepts an offer of gum, drink, or snack, he then proceeds to unzip the fanny pack while assuring that the victim is watching with anticipation. Unfortunately for the anxious victim, an unsuspected visual of a human penis is all that awaits inside the tourists pouch.

"Trumpet"

While in full-chub mode, the arsonist makes a circle by touching the tip of his thumb to the tip of his adjacent index finger. He then proceeds to slide the circle up and down along the shaft of his penis while simultaneously flagellating in a musical sequence. Thus creating a trumpet effect.

"Turtle Power"

This is a very easy attack for an arsonist that is sporting an uncircumcised penis. He simply flashes his penis, in flaccid or sports mode so that the head is still concealed by the foreskin. It is a much more difficult method to execute for those that are circumcised, in which case they must find a way to keep the head of the penis tucked into the skin of the shaft while striking the pose.

"Twizzler"

With the penis in flaccid mode, the arsonist grasps the head of the penis, along with both testicles and twist until they are inner-twined with each other. This is an uncomfortable pose for most attackers, and unattainable for those with insufficient penis length.

"Venus Fly Trap"

This is another very uncomfortable technique to execute. It is similar to the "Castration" technique, but the arsonist must take measures a step further. Instead of just tucking the testicles between his legs, he must also grasp them between his butt-cheeks, as if the testicles are caught up in a Venus fly-trap. This method may require the arsonist to have a more elastic testicle skin than normal, and may prove to be impossible for those with smaller than average sized testicles.

"Voyeur" *

This is a burn, on any random stranger, which enables the arsonist to earn combo points when he is exerting an attack on someone that he does not know.

Chapter 3

3rd Degree Burns

"Anti-Christ" *

A burn attack that is executed within a Christian church building.

"Courtroom" *

A burn attack which is executed in a court of law.

"Devil's Advocate" *

A burn attack that is executed during a religious service.

"False I.D."

Very few have the courage to pull off this attack, and even fewer are willing to endure the consequences. After performing some type of illegal traffic violation to gain the attention of law enforcement, the arsonist pulls over on the shoulder of the road. As part of standard traffic stop procedure, the officer approaches the vehicle to request a valid form of identification from the driver. To the officer's dismay, as he looks down into the driver's lap, instead of a valid driver's license, his eyes are greeted with a humiliating visual of the arsonist's manhood. This method rewards big points for the daring arsonist, but he will more than likely be spending the night in jail.

"Family Portrait" *

This one is certain to cause turmoil within the family circle. While the rest of the family is riddled with anticipation, preparing to make a pleasant lifetime memory at the local photo studio, the arsonist is plotting his fierce attack. Aunts, uncles, cousins, sons, daughters, parents, and grandparents are all oblivious to the humiliation that they are about to endure. As they prepare to smile for their family portrait, the arsonist, disguised as a photographer, strikes his pose of choice and shouts "say cheese!" to the group, rendering the entire flabbergasted family with a third degree burn.

"Grim Reaper" *

A burn attack which is executed during a funeral service.

"Hitch-hiker" *

With traffic at his back, while walking at a brisk pace, and his thumb held out to his side, the arsonist assumes the role of a drifter in search of a hospitable passer-by to give him a lift. As the oncoming vehicles get close enough to recognize his posture, he quickly turns and engages the infamous hitch-hicker's "backwards strut", at which time the oncoming motorist realizes that they have been set up for a third degree burn. The arsonist had already unzipped the front of his pants so that his penis was exposed and ready to inflict injury. Voyeur combo points are usually awarded for this maneuver as the arsonist will normally be unfamiliar with his victim.

"Presidential"

In one of the most respected and difficult burn attempts possible, an arsonist successfully completes an attack on the president of an entire country.

"Rocket Man" *

A burn attack which is executed on a space shuttle while in flight/orbit.

"Sand Castle"

This is a very tough method to accomplish, which is why it is worthy of third degree burn points. The arsonist must first bury his entire body, with the exception of his head and penis, in the sand. This is usually done using an accomplice, thus gaining additional combo points. The level of difficulty comes into play when the arsonist must obtain a full erection so that the penis stands straight in the air, like a sand castle. The "hat trick" can also be implemented in this attack to help render the element of surprise.

"Scrooge" *

Christmas time can present several new burn opportunities for the arsonist that is looking to branch out from the normal standard attacks. One of the all-time holiday favorites is the caroler burn, better known as "scrooge". While church groups are anxiously assembling their teams of cheerful, charismatic songbirds, the arsonist awaits in the quiet of his home for his moment to strike. Door to door the carolers advance in their attempts to spread the Christmas spirit throughout the land. All is merry and bright as they proceed to ring the doorbell for their next audience, but little do they know, that they are about to become spectators to a lethal performance themselves. As the door opens, the group relays their seasons greeting to the tenant, but to their horrible dismay, they are welcomed by a life-altering attack from a less-than-hospitable holiday scrooge. This method is capable of producing multiple combo bonus points.

"Trick Or Treat"

This method can only be executed on Halloween night, October 31st, once each year. The arsonist gets into costume and poses as a child trick-or-treating. He cuts a hole in his candy bag on the side that is facing his genital area. He then places his penis through the hole, and proceeds to ring the doorbell of his soon-to-be victim. The victim/tenant then opens the door at which time the arsonist cheerfully shouts "trick or treat", but as he opens the candy bag to accept the victim's gift, the victim receives a horrific treat of their own, in the form of a gruesome holiday burn.

"Under Oath" *

A burn attack which is executed in a court of law, while on the witness stand. (The arsonist does not gain points for "Courtroom" using this method)

Code of Ethics/ Regulations:

1. Use of force is not prohibited during ANY attack.

2. Children are immune to and protected from attacks. ANY attack on a child (regardless of intent) will PERMANENTLY disqualify the offender.

3. Any physical/bodily harm or injury invoked upon a human (other than the arsonist) or animal during an attack will automatically cancel any earned points during the specific attack.

4. "Official" points shall only be awarded for burn methods mentioned in the current by-laws. (Volume 1)

5. Physical contact is not prohibited during ANY attack.

6. In the case of a victim disputing a burn attempt, an eyewitness can be deferred to. If there are no eyewitnesses to defer to, the burn will not count. The burn will count, however, if the victim does not protest.

Glossary

Arsonist: The person whom is inflicting the burn attack.

Burn: The act of one person forcing another to look at various obscene poses. (Usually executed by way of deceit or the element of surprise.)

Combo: When two or more burn methods are used during an attack.

Choad: The area of flesh located between the testicles and the anal cavity. It is often referred to as the "taint meat" as well.

Chub Mode: A full erection. The penis has increased to its maximum size and is ready for sexual engagement.

Flaccid Mode: The normal inactive state of the penis. No sexual arousal.

Semi-Chub Mode: Partial increase of blood flow to the penis. The beginning stages of "Chub Mode". Penis has begun to increase in length and girth, but is not fully erect.

Sports Mode: A penis that has dramatically decreased in length and girth due to factors such as cold temperatures and tight underwear. A penis that is in a sports mode state can sometimes give the illusion, and feel like, that it is retracting into a man's genital region.

Victim: The person whom is on the receiving end of a burn attack.

* methods that automatically constitute bonus combo credit

Points/Scoring

Although many participants may create there own scoring methods based upon specific relative variables, the official points/scoring system classifies each burn method as 1st, 2nd, or 3rd, degree burn based on the level of difficulty and audacity required to execute:

- 1st degree burn = **5 points**
- 2nd degree burn = **50 points**
- 3rd degree burn = **500 points**
- Combo bonus (*) = **25 points**

An arsonist can be rewarded bonus "combo" points if he executes two or more burn methods within the same attack. An additional <u>25</u> points will be credited <u>per</u> method used.

Example: An inmate at a local prison camp burns his bunk-mate using the "Brain" technique. Points will be credited as follows:

"Bunk-mate" **(5 pts.)** + "Brain" **(5 pts.)** + Combo bonus **(25 pts) = 30 pts.**

Ranking

As participants progress in their efforts and hone their skills through experience they will graduate to higher levels at specific point milestones. Arsonists will then earn a new ranking for their upgraded status.

- **Spark plug** (0-999 points)
- **Fire Fly** (1,000-9,999 points)
- **Pyrotech** (10,000-99,999 points)
- **Napalm Dragon** (100,000-999,999 points)
- **Mulciber** (1,000,000 + points)

Fire Fly

Pyrotech

Napalm Dragon

Mulciber

Authors Note

In an age where boldness is held in high regards and humility has taken a backseat to self-absorbed anarchism, it is easy for the "Burn Game" to be categorized as disrespectful, juvenile, and a non-productive means of spending one's time. These accusations will prove to be 100% correct, yet those that make them are missing the entire objective of this game. I urge those who patronize the "Burn Game" to open there minds to an alternative form of free entertainment that promotes camaraderie and laughter in times of hardship and boredom.

The "Burn Game" is not intended to cause physical or emotional harm to any living or non-living matter in the Universe. All participants are responsible for their own actions, advised to use common sense when executing an attack, and to always conduct themselves as safely as possible. At the end of the day, it is JUST a game, and it is JUST for fun! Although it is extremely vulgar in content, it is good in nature.

Special Thanks to

Luis (L-Rod) Rodriguez, Johnny Szwalla, Daniel (DJ) Johnson, David (S-Pain) Spain, James (Church) Upchurch, Van Crocket, and all others not mentioned who have contributed their helpful ideas.

Printed in the United States
By Bookmasters